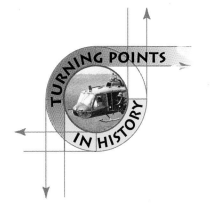

TURNING POINTS IN HISTORY

The Fall of Saigon

The End of the Vietnam War

MICHAEL V USCHAN

Heinemann

www.heinemann.co.uk/library
Visit our website to find out more information about Heinemann Library books.

To order:
☎ Phone 44 (0) 1865 888066
📄 Send a fax to 44 (0) 1865 314091
💻 Visit the Heinemann Bookshop at www.heinemann.co.uk/library to browse our catalogue and order online.

First published in Great Britain by Heinemann Library, Halley Court, Jordan Hill, Oxford OX2 8EJ, a division of Reed Educational and Professional Publishing Ltd. Heinemann is a registered trademark of Reed Educational & Professional Publishing Ltd.

OXFORD MELBOURNE AUCKLAND JOHANNESBURG BLANTYRE
GABORONE IBADAN PORTSMOUTH NH (USA) CHICAGO

Produced for Heinemann Library by Discovery Books Limited
Designed by Sabine Beaupré
Illustrations by Stefan Chabluk
Originated by Ambassador Litho Limited
Printed in Hong Kong

J959.7
1213094

06 05 04 03 02   06 05 04 03
10 9 8 7 6 5 4 3 2 1   10 9 8 7 6 5 4 3 2 1

ISBN 0431 06931 X (hardback)   ISBN 0431 06942 5 (paperback)

British Library Cataloguing in Publication Data

Uschan, Michael V.
The fall of Saigon: the end of the Vietnam War. - (Turning points in history)
1. Vietnamese Conflict, 1961-1975 - Juvenile literature
I. Title
959.7'043

Acknowledgements

The Publishers would like to thank the following for permission to reproduce photographs:
Corbis, pp. 4, 5, 6, 7, 8, 10, 11, 12, 13, 14, 15, 16, 17, 18, 19, 20, 21, 22, 23, 24, 25, 26, 27, 28, 29.

Cover photographs reproduced with permission of Corbis.

Every effort has been made to contact copyright holders of any material reproduced in this book. Any omissions will be rectified in subsequent printings if notice is given to the Publisher.

Contents

Any words appearing in the text in bold, **like this**, are explained in the Glossary.

Surrender in Saigon

The surrender of South Vietnam

Just after midday on 30 April 1975, a new flag was raised over the presidential palace in Saigon, the capital city of South Vietnam. The president, Duong Van Minh, had surrendered to North Vietnam, bringing an end to the Vietnam War.

Fleeing Saigon

Elsewhere in the city, helicopters were landing and taking off from the rooftops, carrying people to safety. Thousands of Saigon residents, fearful for their futures after the defeat, crushed into the United States **embassy** to join American citizens who had clambered onto the roof. In fear of being left behind, people fought brutally to get on the helicopters. It was the largest helicopter **evacuation** in history. In about eighteen hours, starting on 29 April, the aircraft carried nearly 7000 Americans and South Vietnamese to ships waiting offshore.

Some residents of Saigon were afraid that they would be killed when the North Vietnamese took over their city. These people are trying to get into the United States embassy in the hope they will be airlifted to safety by helicopters.

North Vietnam wins

The dramatic helicopter flights were just part of the chaos taking place on the final day of the Vietnam War. At the same time, thousands of soldiers from North Vietnam were rolling into Saigon in tanks and trucks to capture the city.

When Saigon fell, it was clear that the North Vietnamese and the **Vietcong**, their **allies** in South Vietnam, had won the war. As a result, North and South Vietnam were **reunited**.

A war that shook the world

But the war had killed more than two million people and caused problems and conflict around the world. The Vietnam War had raged for 20 years. North Vietnam had received support from its allies, the Soviet Union and China. Soldiers from other nations, including over 50,000 Australians, had helped South Vietnam. South Korea had also sent thousands of soldiers to fight on behalf of South Vietnam. And over the years, the USA sent nearly three million men to support South Vietnam, an action that changed both countries forever.

Victorious North Vietnamese soldiers enter Saigon in April 1975 as the city falls and South Vietnam surrenders at last.

A nation yearning for freedom

Colonial powers

In the 19th century, the UK, France, Germany and other strong nations were colonial powers. This means they took control of weaker countries. They did this to make their nations seem more important, to gain control of certain areas around the world, and to compete with other colonial powers. The colonialists also benefited from the **natural resources** of their **colonies**. These resources were used to make goods that were sold to other nations to create wealth for the colonialists.

Life in rural Vietnam is based around rice cultivation and peasant farming. In some ways the country remains the same as it has been for centuries.

A French colony

In the second half of the 19th century, France seized control of Vietnam and its neighbours Laos and Cambodia. France governed these three countries in south-east Asia as the colony of French Indochina.

Vietnam's main natural resource was coal. It was also a farming nation, and most Vietnamese were peasant farmers who lived in small villages and grew rice.

Unhappy Vietnamese

Vietnam was part of the French empire from 1883 until 1954. Many Vietnamese were angry that another nation ruled them. The French made all the laws, profited the most from the **economy** and **exploited** the poorer Vietnamese.

In the early years of the 20th century, many Vietnamese began to demand their independence. One was Nguyen Tat Thanh, born in 1890. He later became known as Ho Chi Minh, a name that means 'he who **enlightens**'. Ho Chi Minh believed in nationalism, or the right of citizens to rule their country without interference. He also became a **communist** in the 1920s.

When World War I ended in 1918, US President Woodrow Wilson tried to put a stop to colonialism by supporting **self-determination** for all nations. Wilson said, 'people [should] be governed only by their own consent'. In 1919, at an international peace conference after World War I, Ho Chi Minh made an appeal for **reform** in Vietnam. But France wanted to keep its colonies, and his request was denied by the USA and powerful European nations. However, Ho Chi Minh would keep fighting for his nation's freedom.

European colonialists in the 19th century often used the strength of their superior armies and weapons to take over other parts of the world. Here, the victorious French enter Hanoi, the capital of Vietnam.

VIETNAM'S LONG HISTORY

Vietnam is an ancient land. It first emerged as an independent kingdom called Nam Viet in about 200 BCE. For much of its history, however, it was dominated by bigger and stronger nations. China, its powerful northern neighbour, conquered Vietnam in 111 BCE and ruled it for more than a thousand years. The country became independent again in 939 CE, when the Vietnamese general Ngo Quyen drove out the Chinese.

Vietnam defeats France

The elephant and the grasshopper

'The elephant and the grasshopper' is the way Ho Chi Minh described the battle for his nation's independence. France, a powerful European nation, was the 'elephant' while his small band of soldiers was the 'grasshopper'. Yet, in the end, the grasshopper would overcome the elephant.

Ho declares independence

In 1940, during World War II, the French surrendered control of their **colony** to Japan when the Japanese invaded French Indochina. Ho Chi Minh then saw a chance to free his country. He created the League for the Independence of Vietnam, also called the Vietminh. The Vietminh began fighting the Japanese and successfully resisted the invasion. On 2 September 1945, Ho Chi Minh gave a speech that proclaimed his nation's freedom. He borrowed a key phrase from the American Declaration of Independence when he said, 'all men are created equal'.

Dien Bien Phu

The French had never treated the Vietnamese as equals, and they wanted to regain control of Vietnam. In 1946 Ho Chi Minh and the Vietminh began to fight against French forces for their independence. France was supported with money and help by the USA, and also by some Vietnamese. The war continued

French soldiers withdraw from the Vietnamese capital Hanoi in 1954, after the Vietnamese won the battle at Dien Bien Phu.

for years. Finally, in May 1954, a decisive event took place at Dien Bien Phu, a village in north-west Vietnam. There, over 10,000 French soldiers surrendered after a 55-day siege. France decided to withdraw its forces from Indochina after the defeat.

A country divided

Ho thought Vietnam had won its independence and would now be free from foreign interference. But when the USA and other nations met in Geneva, Switzerland, to decide peace terms, Ho's dream was shattered. On 21 July 1954, the nations approved the Geneva Accords. This agreement divided the country into two nations, North Vietnam and South Vietnam. Saigon became capital of the South, Hanoi capital of the North.

The reason for this division was that Vietnam's fight for independence had become part of the Cold War. This was a battle for control after World War II between the **communist** Soviet Union and the **capitalist** USA. Ho Chi Minh became leader of the communist-supported North Vietnam. South Vietnam was supported by capitalist nations.

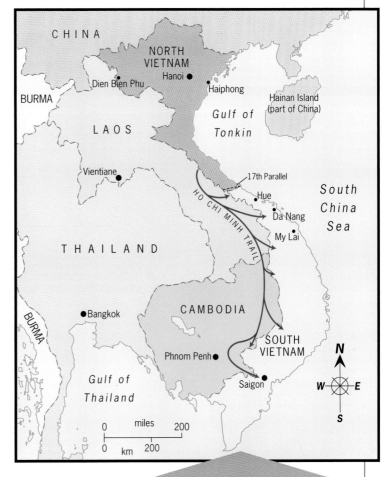

This map shows Vietnam and its neighbours Laos and Cambodia, also once part of French Indochina. When Vietnam was split, North Vietnam was backed by another neighbour, the large, communist nation of China.

The USA gets involved

Fighting communism

Americans in the 1950s greatly feared **communism** because they believed it was a system that denied people freedom. The USA's leaders believed in containment, the need to keep communism from spreading from one nation to another. Between 1950 and 1954, the USA gave France US$2.6 billion to fight against communism in Indochina.

When the French were defeated in 1954, US President Dwight Eisenhower decided America had to continue opposing communism in Vietnam. Ngo Dinh Diem was chosen as president of South Vietnam. South Vietnam was backed by the USA. From 1954 to 1963, the USA gave South Vietnam about another US$1.7 billion in aid.

John Kennedy (right), soon to be president of the USA, visits President Eisenhower at the White House in 1960. Eisenhower had been supporting South Vietnam with soldiers and money for several years. Now the conflict was to become Kennedy's problem.

No fair election

The Geneva Accords had said the split into North and South was temporary, and that there should be a fair election after two years to choose a government to **reunite** Vietnam. North Vietnam did hold elections and chose Ho Chi Minh as president. Ngo Dinh Diem, however, refused to hold an election in South Vietnam because he and his US supporters feared that Ho Chi Minh would win. On 26 October 1955, Diem declared himself president of South Vietnam without elections.

War begins

Diem's decision caused anger in the North and amongst those in South Vietnam who opposed Diem's rule. In the mid-1950s, the communists and other supporters of Ho Chi Minh began fighting to overthrow South Vietnam's government. The Vietminh **allied** themselves with the communist government of North Vietnam and were reorganized as the **Vietcong**. They also received aid from the communist governments of the Soviet Union and China.

Meanwhile, starting in 1955, President Dwight Eisenhower and his successor President John Kennedy began sending 'military advisers' (soldiers) to support South Vietnam and train its army to fight better. The Vietnam War had begun.

THE FREE WORLD

American leaders after World War II were afraid that if one country in south-east Asia became communist, others would follow. This was called the 'domino theory'. John Kennedy claimed South Vietnam was important as 'the cornerstone of the free world in south-east Asia' after he was elected president in 1960.

The Chinese leader Mao Zedong (left) was a powerful communist who supported Ho Chi Minh (right). The two leaders are at a banquet held in Ho Chi Minh's honour in China in 1955.

A guerrilla war

The Vietcong

The Vietnam War started as a civil war, a war in which citizens of a country fight against each other. The conflict was mainly a **guerrilla** war. In this type of fighting, there are no large armies meeting on the battlefield. Instead, small groups of soldiers act on their own, making surprise attacks.

The **Vietcong** lived in rural villages and had control of the countryside. From their **strongholds**, they fought the South Vietnamese army and engaged in terrorism. Vietcong death squads killed tens of thousands of national, local and village officials. They exploded bombs in cities, where the South Vietnamese and their **allies** were in control. It was not hard for the Vietcong to target their enemies in the cities and army encampments. But it was difficult for the South Vietnamese to track down or fight the Vietcong because it was almost impossible to tell them apart from the villagers they lived with.

The rule of Ngo Dinh Diem was harsh on many South Vietnamese. Diem was a Roman Catholic and persecuted **Buddhists**, such as these monks drying rice outside their temple. Some Buddhist monks even burned themselves alive in protest at restrictions Diem placed on their religious life.

Weak South Vietnam

In spite of the growth in American aid to the South, the **communists** were winning the battle for Vietnam. By 1962, the Vietcong's fierce guerrilla warfare had given them control of much of South Vietnam's rural areas.

A mother takes shelter with her baby in a canal bank near her village. The South Vietnamese soldiers passing by have just reclaimed the village from a group of Vietcong guerrillas.

Another reason the Vietcong were successful was that Ngo Dinh Diem governed South Vietnam brutally and badly. He gave a lot of power to his family members, and many of his government officials were corrupt: they stole money and supplies that should have gone to help people. Generally, the South Vietnamese hated the way Diem ruled their country. On 1 November 1963, Diem was shot and killed in a military takeover.

Another assassination

Fearing a communist victory, President Kennedy had greatly increased the number of military advisers to South Vietnam in 1962 and 1963. By 1963, some 16,000 American soldiers were there. However, Kennedy had criticized Diem's regime and questioned the USA's role in Vietnam. Some historians believe Kennedy would have withdrawn all American troops in a year or two. Others disagree. But on 22 November 1963, Kennedy was shot and killed by an assassin in Texas.

A SOLDIER'S DUTY

A Vietcong soldier wrote this to his girlfriend during the Vietnam War: *'Before, I did not know what it was like to kill a man; now that I have seen it, I don't want to do it anymore. But it is the duty of a soldier to die for his country, me for our fatherland, the enemy for his. There is no choice.'*

America escalates the war

President Lyndon Johnson

Vice President Lyndon Johnson became president when John Kennedy was assassinated. Johnson wanted to save South Vietnam from **communism**, but the **Vietcong** grew stronger and stepped up their actions after Diem was killed. Johnson decided America had to do more to help South Vietnam.

A troop-ship crammed with American soldiers arrives in Vietnam. By 1968 there were 536,000 Americans fighting in the Vietnam War.

He soon got his chance. In August 1964 a North Vietnamese patrol boat fired on the US destroyer *Maddox* that was on a secret operation in the Gulf of Tonkin, off the coast of North Vietnam. The ship was not harmed, but the event gave President Johnson enough reason to ask the American government for more power to fight the war. **Congress** quickly passed the Gulf of Tonkin Resolution. This gave the president the right to **escalate** the USA's role in the war by sending more troops to Vietnam and 'to take all necessary measures to repel any armed attack against forces of the United States'.

American might

In 1964 there were only 23,000 United States troops in Vietnam. A year later that number had grown to 184,000. The South Vietnamese forces also grew dramatically, from 243,000 in 1963, to 820,000 by 1968, and eventually to more than a million.

Operation Rolling Thunder

In addition to full-scale ground combat, in March 1965 the USA began bombing North Vietnam from the air. The bombing attacks were known as 'Operation Rolling Thunder'. American aeroplanes dropped eight million tonnes of bombs. Many were **napalm** bombs, which instantly set fire to the land where they fell. They destroyed huge areas of countryside and killed and wounded many people.

US Phantom planes release their bombs over targets in North Vietnam. In Operation Rolling Thunder, the USA dropped three times the amount of bombs dropped in all of World War II.

No end in sight

Search and destroy

The American **escalation** of the war continued from 1965 to 1968. One reason the war dragged on was that American forces had trouble just finding the enemy in the remote, wooded areas they inhabited. In **search and destroy** missions, Americans had first to hunt down the **Vietcong** before they could attack. These search and destroy missions often devastated the homes and lives of innocent South Vietnamese.

Death and deception

Powerful aeroplanes, superior weapons and helicopters that could rush soldiers into battle helped US forces kill a lot of **communist** soldiers. The USA began issuing body counts, which were lists of the number of enemy soldiers it had killed. However, US officials falsely increased these numbers to make it appear as if the USA was winning the war. Meanwhile, the number of American fatalities also grew rapidly. Despite pouring billions of dollars and many soldiers into the war, the USA could not defeat the communists.

A door gunner in a 'Huey' helicopter opens fire on a target he has sighted below. The helicopter was part of an attack squadron on a search and destroy mission.

Hue, Vietnam's cultural and religious centre, was one of the towns and cities attacked in the Tet Offensive. Here, American **Marines** in Hue take cover behind their tank after being fired on by Vietcong. Most of Hue was destroyed in less than a month.

The Tet Offensive

In 1968, a week-long truce was announced to observe Tet, the Vietnamese New Year. On 30 January 1968, completely ignoring the agreement, some 70,000 Vietcong and North Vietnamese launched one of the war's fiercest **offensives**. They struck 36 major towns and cities throughout South Vietnam and terrorized the entire nation. The attacks went on for several weeks and became known as the Tet Offensive. American and South Vietnamese forces eventually defeated the attackers, but many people now did not believe the communists could be beaten. It was an important turning point in the progress of the Vietnam War.

INNOCENT VICTIMS

People all over the world began to question the Vietnam War, because thousands of innocent citizens were killed. Soldiers sometimes mistakenly shot people who were not communists. The worst known incident happened on 16 March 1968 in a village called My Lai. At least 175, and maybe as many as 450, unarmed civilians, including children, were killed by American soldiers. The victims were innocent villagers, and the commander of the soldiers was later convicted of murder. A villager who survived the massacre at My Lai later said, *'It's why I'm old before my time. … I won't forgive as long as I live. Think of the babies being killed, then ask me why I hate them* [the Americans].'

An unpopular war

The war on television

The Vietnam War was the first war to be shown on television throughout the world. Daily news stories brought the conflict directly into people's homes. The news helped shape public opinion by giving people a closer look at war than they had ever had. They could see for themselves what was happening rather than relying on official reports. In January 1968, people were stunned by images of the Tet Offensive. It showed that US officials were not providing all the facts when they claimed that the **communists** were being defeated.

Anti-war protesters

All over the world, protest at American involvement in Vietnam increased as the years went by. Americans, at first, were united in helping South Vietnam. But as the USA's involvement in the war **escalated** they, too, began to oppose the war. One reason was the **draft**. This forced young men to join the armed forces and fight in Vietnam even if they opposed the war. And thousands of them were being killed.

A priest gives comfort to a dying **Marine** after an attack by North Vietnamese. Pictures like these were seen around the world. They made people question why lives were being lost in Vietnam.

Anti-war protests spread through American universities in 1965. In the following years, millions of people in the USA and elsewhere participated in all kinds of protests. There were huge marches and demonstrations in New York, San Francisco and Washington, DC, in 1967.

Richard Nixon takes over

President Johnson became very unpopular as a result of his administration's policies of escalating the war and increasing the American presence in Vietnam. He decided not to stand for re-election when the elections came around in 1968. The presidency was won by Richard Nixon.

A crowd gathers in Washington, DC, to oppose the Vietnam War. Demonstrators hold up a large peace sign that became a familiar symbol of protest during the war years.

Protestors are shot

In May 1970, widespread protests about American involvement in the war took place at American universities. The protests turned to tragedy when four students were shot and killed at Kent State University in Ohio and two more died at Jackson State College in Mississippi. They died in clashes with policemen and soldiers who were trying to stop the demonstrations. That spring, about 400 universities were shut down at least temporarily because of the violence.

From battlefield to peace talks

Vietnamization

President Nixon continued sending Americans to fight in Vietnam. But he also began a process he called 'Vietnamization' of the war. This meant making South Vietnam strong enough to defeat the **communists** without the support of American forces. Then, Nixon could decrease the US presence in Vietnam.

In 1969, Nixon dramatically increased aid to South Vietnam in the form of military equipment and more advisers to train the South Vietnamese. At the same time, he announced the first withdrawal of American troops. Their number dropped by over 60,000 in 1969.

The main negotiators between the USA and North Vietnam were Henry Kissinger (front right) and Le Duc Tho (front left). Many people believe it is because of Kissinger that the USA finally managed to withdraw from Vietnam.

The bombing continues

The USA was reducing its presence in Vietnam, but President Nixon extended the area of the war. For several years the North Vietnamese had sent soldiers and supplies through Cambodia and Laos along a route known as the Ho Chi Minh Trail (see map on page 9). In 1970–71, the US attacked communist **strongholds** along the Cambodian border and the Ho Chi Minh Trail in Laos, cutting off supplies and refuge for the communists.

By 1971, the number of Americans in Vietnam had dropped to under 160,000. South Vietnamese soldiers did most of the fighting while the US provided them with air support and continued bombing attacks.

Peace talks

Another of President Nixon's **policies** was to pursue peace talks with North Vietnam. In May 1968, under President Johnson, American representatives had first met with North Vietnamese officials in Paris to negotiate a peaceful end to the war. The talks continued on and off for several years, both publicly and secretly.

During this time, the fighting continued and sometimes even intensified. In spite of this, a peace agreement was finally reached on 27 January 1973. The Paris Peace Accords were signed by North Vietnam, South Vietnam, the USA and the **Vietcong**. The agreement called for a complete cease-fire and for the USA to withdraw all its soldiers from Vietnam. It also said that foreign military activity should stop in Laos and Cambodia. For the future, it was agreed that Vietnam should receive **economic** aid; that elections should be held in South Vietnam; and that North and South should work together for **reconciliation**.

Captain Michael Kerr arrives home to his family in 1973. He had been a prisoner of war in Vietnam since his aeroplane was shot down in 1967. Nearly 600 American prisoners of war held in Vietnam were released as part of the 1973 peace agreement.

After the agreement

Unfortunately, the USA's withdrawal was the only part of the peace agreement that worked. The last US troops left Vietnam on 29 March 1973, but fighting between North and South Vietnam continued for two more years.

The fall of Saigon

The fighting continues

After the American withdrawal, the South Vietnamese army tried to keep its country from being conquered by the **Vietcong** and North Vietnam. The USA continued to give money and equipment to South Vietnam. But resisting the **communist** forces was a difficult task without the support of American troops.

For two years, there were no huge gains on either side. In January 1975, however, the collapse of South Vietnam began as attacks on the nation's northern and coastal regions caused the South Vietnamese to retreat further and further south. The North Vietnamese steadily gained ground.

The last days

On 29 April 1975, North Vietnamese soldiers who had surrounded Saigon began firing artillery shells into the city. The explosions signalled South Vietnam's final days of existence.

In the previous few weeks, USA officials in Saigon had **evacuated** 120,000 South Vietnamese. These

On a rooftop in Saigon, an American government employee helps a line of terrified Vietnamese into an American helicopter that will airlift them out of the city.

refugees feared the communists would kill them or put them in prison for having supported the South Vietnamese government. As the fall of Saigon loomed, the USA also evacuated 20,000 American citizens. Most of these were government employees and their families.

The last people to leave were taken by helicopter from the roof of the United States **embassy** and other sites to ships waiting in the South China Sea. 'The roof of the embassy was a vision out of a nightmare,' said American government employee Frank Snepp.

Refugees crowded into the port at Saigon as the city fell to North Vietnam. They hoped to be taken to safety by the Americans.

Ho Chi Minh City

The evacuation ended when communist troops entered Saigon. On 30 April, South Vietnamese President Duong Van Minh announced the unconditional surrender of the Saigon government. The war was over and the communists had won.

Saigon got a new name as well as a new government. The city would now be called Ho Chi Minh City after the legendary leader who, over 50 years earlier, had started fighting for Vietnam's independence. Ho had died in 1969 after ten years of declining health.

DEATHS IN THE VIETNAM WAR

North and South Vietnamese civilians	over 1,000,000
North Vietnamese and Vietcong troops	about 900,000
South Vietnamese troops	about 200,000
American civilians and troops	about 58,000
Australian troops	about 500

Vietnam after reunification

North and south reunited

When the North Vietnamese took over the South, they combined the two parts of Vietnam into one country. In April 1976, voters throughout Vietnam elected representatives to form a new government. On 2 July 1976, the two Vietnams were officially **reunited**. The new nation was named the Socialist Republic of Vietnam.

Re-education camps

Many people fled South Vietnam because they thought the **communists** would kill those who had opposed them. As it turned out, there were no immediate mass executions as had been feared. But hundreds of thousands of people were sent to 're-education' camps and forced to become believers in communism. Many people in the camps were treated inhumanely and some were tortured and killed.

All over Vietnam, from tiny villages to large cities, homes were destroyed. In Saigon, seen here after a bombing attack, thousands were left homeless.

War's devastation

The war had caused unbelievable damage in Vietnam. Bombs had flattened large sections of major cities. American aeroplanes had also sprayed nearly 72 million litres of herbicides – chemicals that kill plants – to destroy the thick foliage of the rainforest that hid communist soldiers, and the rice crops that fed them.

The herbicides had further, lasting effects. They polluted large areas of farmland, making them unusable for years. The chemicals – such as the widely-used Agent Orange – also caused fatal diseases in those who were exposed to them, including the US soldiers who had done the spraying.

There were other dangers that did not disappear. Thousands of land-mines that had been buried by both sides continued to explode, killing and injuring innocent people.

A long recovery

The war shattered Vietnam's **economy**. It is still one of the world's poorest and least advanced nations. Most Vietnamese live in poverty and their systems of education, healthcare and technology are far below those enjoyed by other people throughout the world.

Millions of people fled South Vietnam and became **refugees**. Many thousands, known as the 'Vietnamese boat people' because they arrived in boats, came to Hong Kong from Vietnam. But there was nowhere to house them except in camps such as this one.

VIETNAM'S NEIGHBOURS

The fall of Saigon was a turning point for Vietnam's neighbours, too. The government of Cambodia surrendered to the communist-led Khmer Rouge at the same time as communists were occupying South Vietnam. And in Laos, communists soon took control without any bloodshed.

America after the Vietnam War

First loss

The fall of Saigon was a symbolic defeat for the USA that was seen on television screens around the world. Not only had its military forces earlier failed to win in Vietnam, but Saigon's surrender was a political disaster. The fall of Saigon had shown that the USA had been unable to defeat **communism**.

For a time after the Vietnam War, the USA avoided any large-scale **intervention** in foreign conflicts. The general feeling was that a large and costly mistake had been made, and it must not be repeated.

Economic problems

The USA spent an estimated US$167 billion on the Vietnam War. Because it cost more to fight the war each year than it received in taxes, America had to borrow billions of dollars. The debt caused **economic** problems and unemployment in the USA for several years.

President Nixon appeared on television in 1970 to tell the nation why he had ordered American attacks on Cambodia, Vietnam's neighbour. During the course of the Vietnam War, Americans learned to question their leaders' decisions.

Loss of faith

Americans also lost faith in their leaders, who had lied to them during the war. In 1973 **Congress** passed the War Powers Act, which said that from then on presidents had to get approval from Congress each time they sent troops into action overseas. Americans hoped this would prevent further unnecessary bloodshed.

Vietnam had been the first 'television war', and television had revealed how the public had been misled. After the fall of Saigon, the USA and other governments would always be more carefully watched by television and newspapers, and the public would know more about what their leaders were doing.

Other effects

Many soldiers returned home suffering from physical injuries, mental trauma or drug problems. At first, some Americans appeared to reject the returning **veterans**, wrongly blaming them for the mistakes of government. It took a while before those who had served through the horrors of war received the recognition they deserved.

The war also changed the population of America because more than one million south-east Asians, including about 700,000 Vietnamese, fled communism by emigrating there. Many **refugees** who feared living under communist rule found a better life in the USA.

DAMAGE DONE

Former US Defence Secretary Robert McNamara helped plan the Vietnam War. Years later, he admitted the war had harmed his country. He said, *'By the time the United States finally left South Vietnam in 1973, we had lost 58,000 men and women; our economy had been damaged by years of heavy and improperly financed war spending; and the political unity of our society had been shattered, not to be restored for decades.'*

Veterans of the Vietnam War gather every year on Veteran's Day at the Vietnam Memorial in Washington, DC. There they are honoured for their service and remember those who died in the war.

The world after the fall of Saigon

The effect of communist victory

Contrary to the domino theory, the fall of Saigon did not lead to **communism** sweeping though south-east Asia. But the victories in Vietnam, first against France and then against the USA, gave hope to other nations that were being forcibly ruled. Citizens of **dictatorships**, **colonies**, and eventually even communist countries, increasingly fought for freedom.

How the world saw the USA

Many smaller nations continued to look to America for support in protecting their freedom. But indecision by the world's most powerful nation affected many countries. In the 1990s, the USA hesitated to respond to the conflict in Yugoslavia, and many Americans opposed **intervention**.

In 2000, Vietnam and the USA signed a trade agreement, something that never would have happened during the Cold War. As a result, American businesses are building factories such as this one in Vietnam.

On the other hand, after the Vietnam War, many nations became suspicious of American intervention abroad and remained so. The USA's **allies** in Europe, for instance, had never supported American involvement in Vietnam. And the USA's relationship with China continued to be unstable.

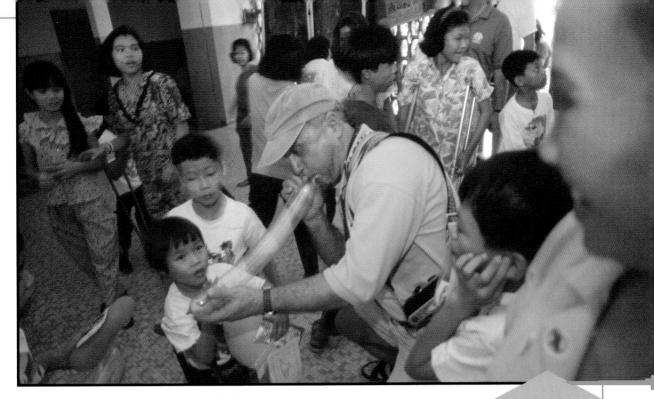

The end of the Cold War

The Vietnam War was an extension of the Cold War between the USA and the Soviet Union. After the fall of Saigon, the Soviets continued giving Vietnam about US$1 billion in **economic** and military aid each year. The huge amounts of money spent by the Soviet Union to support Vietnam and other communist nations helped to weaken its own economy. And economic problems, more than anything else, led to the Soviet Union's collapse in the early 1990s. And this in turn brought about the end of the Cold War.

The USA and Vietnam

The break-up of the Soviet Union eased American fears about communism. This made it easier for the USA and Vietnam finally to resume peaceful relations. In November 2000, President Bill Clinton became the first president to visit Vietnam since Nixon in 1969. Clinton proposed the two countries should work together for a better future. 'Once we met here as adversaries [enemies],' he said. 'Today, we work as partners.'

An American **veteran** of the Vietnam War visits this orphanage in Ho Chi Minh City (formerly Saigon) twice a year. As well as entertaining the children, he brings money and medicine that is so badly needed.

Time-line

1883–1954	Vietnam ruled by France as part of French Indochina
1945	2 September – Ho Chi Minh declares Vietnam independent
1946–54	Vietminh fight French forces for control of Vietnam
1950–54	USA provides military and economic aid to French to fight communism in Indochina
1954	7 May – communist forces defeat French at Dien Bien Phu 21 July – Geneva Accords divide Vietnam into North and South
1955	23 February – first US military advisers sent to Vietnam April – fighting begins as Vietcong and North Vietnamese try to overthrow government of South Vietnam 26 October – Ngo Dinh Diem declares himself president of South Vietnam without elections
1960	November – John Kennedy elected president of USA
1962–63	President Kennedy greatly increases US military presence in Vietnam
1963	1 November – South Vietnamese President Ngo Dinh Diem assassinated 22 November – John Kennedy assassinated and Lyndon Johnson becomes president of USA
1964	2 August – US destroyer *Maddox* attacked in Gulf of Tonkin 4 August – Congress approves Gulf of Tonkin Resolution
1965	7 February – President Johnson orders bombing of North Vietnam
1968	30 January – North Vietnamese and Vietcong launch Tet Offensive 16 March – between 175 and 450 unarmed civilians killed in My Lai Massacre May – First peace talks November – Richard Nixon elected president of USA
1969	Vietnamization begins First withdrawal of US troops from Vietnam 3 September – Ho Chi Minh dies
1970	Six students killed in anti-war protests in USA
1973	27 January – Paris Peace Accords signed 29 March – last US troops leave South Vietnam US Congress passes War Powers Act
1975	30 April – Saigon falls and South Vietnamese government surrenders to communists
1976	2 July – North and South Vietnam reunited as Socialist Republic of Vietnam
2000	Trade agreement between Vietnam and USA November – US President Bill Clinton visits Vietnam

Glossary

ally	friend or supporter in a conflict
Buddhist	follower of the Asian religion of Buddhism, which teaches people to aim for enlightenment and goodness
capitalism	economic system in which private individuals own property and make economic decisions
colony	nation or region ruled by another country
communism	economic and political system in which government controls the economy and citizens have common ownership of property and resources
Congress	elected government of the USA
dictatorship	country ruled by a dictator, a person who takes complete control often without being elected
draft	legal requirement for people to join their country's military forces
economy	resources, such as goods and services, of a nation, and the system of money that controls resources
embassy	office and residence of an ambassador, the person who represents his or her government in a foreign country
enlighten	help show the truth or make something clear
escalate	increase in stages
evacuation	getting people out of a particular area during an emergency
exploit	use or take advantage of people, usually unfairly or cruelly
guerrilla	soldier who fights or attacks as part of small independent group
intervention	getting involved in affairs of other countries
Marine	member of the United States Marine Corps, a branch of the US military forces
napalm	sticky chemical substance that causes things to burn
natural resources	useful materials found in the land, such as fuel (coal, gas and wood), valuable metals (iron and gold) or water
offensive	organized attack on an enemy
policy	decision about the way to do something
reconciliation	the act of getting back together or becoming friends again
reform	change that improves conditions
refugees	people forced to leave their homes
reunite	join back together. When two countries reunite, it is called reunification.
search and destroy	missions to find and kill enemy soldiers
self-determination	right to make decisions about one's own life and country
stronghold	place where group can hide out and store supplies
veteran	person who has served in a war
Vietcong	communist-led army of South Vietnamese formed to fight South Vietnamese government

Index